To my starting five, you are my greatest win.
To my team, thanks for making my dreams come true.

Just Like Caitlin
Copyright © 2024 by Ally Obermeier

ISBN 979-8-2184-2533-3

Illustrated by Makenzie McCarthy
Produced and Designed by Tim Palin Creative
Printed in Canada by Friesens Corporation

JUST LIKE CAITLIN

Written By
**Ally
Obermeier**

Illustrated By
**Makenzie
McCarthy**

Eden looked at the clock.

3...

She took a dribble.

2...

She let the ball fly.

1...

The ball hit the rim and fell to the ground.

Bzzz ...

Eden's team lost. She was mad. She was mad shaking hands with the opposing team. She was mad in her team's post-game huddle. And she was mad taking off her shoes. Eden did not like to lose.

Eden's grandpa was her biggest fan. He was at every game. He came over and said, "Great effort, Eden. That was fun to watch."

Eden scowled. "It wasn't fun for me because we lost."

"I know you love to win, but there's more to life than winning," Grandpa said.

"It doesn't feel that way," Eden said.

Grandpa smiled, "Let's go get a treat. I have a story I want to tell you."

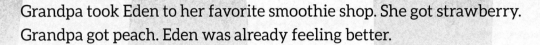

Grandpa took Eden to her favorite smoothie shop. She got strawberry.
Grandpa got peach. Eden was already feeling better.

"There was a girl who was just like you. She loved basketball, and she loved winning," Grandpa said.

Eden smiled. Grandpa told the best stories and always knew exactly what to say to cheer her up.

"Her name was Caitlin Clark. She was born in Des Moines, Iowa," Grandpa said.

"Is that the state with the potatoes?" Eden asked.

"No," Grandpa laughed. "You're thinking of Idaho. Iowa has pigs and corn."

"That's right," Eden said. "Keep going, Grandpa."

"Caitlin grew up with a loving dad, mom, and two brothers. She also lived near lots of family. Playing with family was her favorite, and she was always trying to keep up. Because they all wanted to win, games often ended in tears or arguments. But their love was deep and more important than any game."

"Caitlin never backed down from a challenge. It didn't matter what she was doing, she loved to compete. As Caitlin grew, so did her dreams. She looked up to the stars, watching, learning, and thinking, *One day I want to be just like them.* Basketball became Caitlin's favorite sport. She joined a traveling team and spent hours in the gym. Practices and tournaments were the highlight of her week."

"This does sound just like me, Grandpa," interrupted Eden.

Grandpa smiled. "Caitlin's hard work paid off. She led her team to win their league's biggest tournament. She had talent, and people noticed."

"Caitlin was outstanding in high school. One game she scored sixty points! She set many records, was a high school All-American, and won two gold medals for the United States before graduating."

"Nearly every college wanted Caitlin on their team. Caitlin chose to stay in Iowa. She loved her home state and wanted her family to be at her games. She had big dreams for her college career. And while some people laughed, Caitlin believed in herself."

CAITLIN

"Caitlin made an impact on women's college basketball right away. She led the country in scoring her first two seasons. She played with joy and a passion to win."

"But a new team and new coach took adjusting to, and things weren't always perfect. Caitlin didn't like to lose."

"Caitlin's success grew, and her team won the Big Ten Tournament Championship her second year at Iowa. Expectations were high to win many games in the NCAA Tournament. But the Hawkeyes fell short and lost in the second round. A familiar foe ended the Hawkeyes' season in shock."

"I bet Caitlin was so mad," Eden said.

"I bet she was," Grandpa continued. "It was a big disappointment. But instead of staying mad, Caitlin kept dreaming. She never stopped believing."

"Year three was a big one for Caitlin. People loved watching her because she surprised them. Others who had never shown interest in women's college basketball began to watch. She led her team to win another Big Ten Tournament Championship. That year, the NCAA Tournament would be much different."

"The Hawkeyes beat one tough opponent after another. Only one team stood between them and Caitlin's dream. The opposing team got out to a fast start. But when the Hawkeyes took the lead, they never looked back."

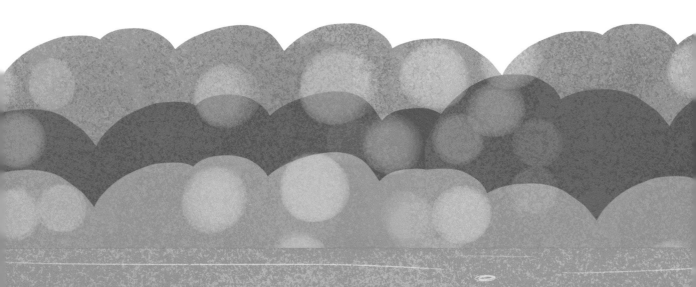

"The Hawkeyes made it to the biggest stage in women's college basketball. A sea of black and gold showed up to cheer them on. An undefeated basketball giant stood ready to battle."

"The game went back and forth until the very end ... and the Hawkeyes won! Few people thought the Hawkeyes could win, but Caitlin and her team believed they would. They defeated the highest-ranked team and earned a ticket to the national championship game."

"Fans old and new tuned in to watch. It was an exciting match-up in front of a sold-out crowd. The Hawkeyes were ready for the challenge. It was a competitive game, and Caitlin led everyone in scoring. But her team came up a few points short and ended the season in second place."

"The Hawkeyes were heartbroken, really wanting to win for themselves and the state of Iowa. Yet they held their heads high and were proud of what they accomplished. It could have been easy for them to be mad. But the way they handled the loss spoke louder about their character than any win could."

"I want my legacy to be the impact that I have on young kids and the people in the state of Iowa. I hope I brought them a lot of joy this season."

-Caitlin Clark

"Caitlin's fourth and final year at Iowa arrived. With it came an excitement unlike anything women's college basketball had seen. The Hawks sold out every arena they played in. People came from miles around to watch Caitlin and her teammates play."

"Caitlin was growing the game, and the numbers showed it. It became hard to keep track of all the records broken that season, except one. Caitlin became the all-time leading scorer in both men's and women's college basketball. She reached a level no one had been before and left her mark in the history books forever."

"The Hawkeyes had another great regular season. Yet many people wondered if they could repeat the success of last year's tournament performance. Those questions were soon answered."

"Caitlin's final Big Ten Tournament did not disappoint. In a very exciting game, the Hawkeyes fought back from a big halftime deficit. Iowa won their third straight Big Ten Tournament Championship!"

"The anticipation surrounding the women's NCAA tournament was off the charts. Iowa won their first three games setting up a rematch against last year's national champion. The talent and toughness displayed by both teams was excellent. But Iowa played with a confidence and control that resulted in a big victory."

"Back-to-back semifinal appearances was a dream come true. But Caitlin wasn't done yet. Iowa faced a historical basketball powerhouse. The Hawks were behind most of the game but never gave up. Every player made big plays to secure the win and a second straight trip to the national title game."

"Millions of people, a record number, watched as Caitlin played her last college game. It was another try at the championship trophy. It was another matchup against the undefeated and top-seeded team. The Hawks got out to a fast start. Caitlin scored 18 points in the first quarter. But they could not hold on to the lead and finished runner-up."

Eden looked sad, "I wish Caitlin and her team would have won. Losing really stinks."

Grandpa responded, "Winning was the goal, and losing is hard. But it did not define them. They gave it their all and were proud of all they had done."

"Caitlin won a ton of awards during her time at Iowa. Many people said she was one of the greatest to play the game. She inspired people to be great through her hard work. She encouraged people to dream big through her confidence."

"Yet this was only part of Caitlin's story. She started her professional career selected as the number one pick in the WNBA draft! But I will have to finish that story another day. It is time for us to get back for your next game."

"Wow, that is an awesome story! I want to be just like Caitlin," Eden said.

Grandpa smiled. "I want you to be just like Caitlin too. She had an amazing basketball career. It was full of crazy records, huge wins, and deserving awards. She lost games and made mistakes too. But she never forgot that the people in her life were more important than the game. She loved to win, but she loved her people more."

Eden gave Grandpa a hug. "I'm glad I got this time with you, Grandpa. You will always mean more to me than basketball."